THIS BOOK BELONGS TO

....

Copyright © 2017

make believe ideas ltd

The Wilderness, Berkhamsted, Hertfordshire, HP4 2AZ, UK.
6th Floor, South Bank House, Barrow Street, Dublin 4, D04 TR29, Ireland.

www.makebelieveideas.co.uk

THE STORY OF
EASTER

Written by Fiona Boon
Illustrated by Dawn Machell

JESUS—SON OF GOD

Jesus came to earth to live life as a man.

He was one of us, a part of God's great plan.

He taught us the truth and what God's love meant.

Many people followed Him everywhere He went.

THE LAST SUPPER

JESUS AND THE PEOPLE

One day, on a donkey, He entered a **great** town.

His followers all **cheered**, but some men wore a **frown**.

These men **hated** Jesus and all that He had done.

They were **cross** when Jesus said He was God's own **son**.

THE LAST SUPPER

Jesus shared a supper with all His closest friends.

He knew His time on earth was coming to an end.

JESUS PRAYS

He went into a garden late that night to pray.

Desperate, He said, "Father, is this the only way?"

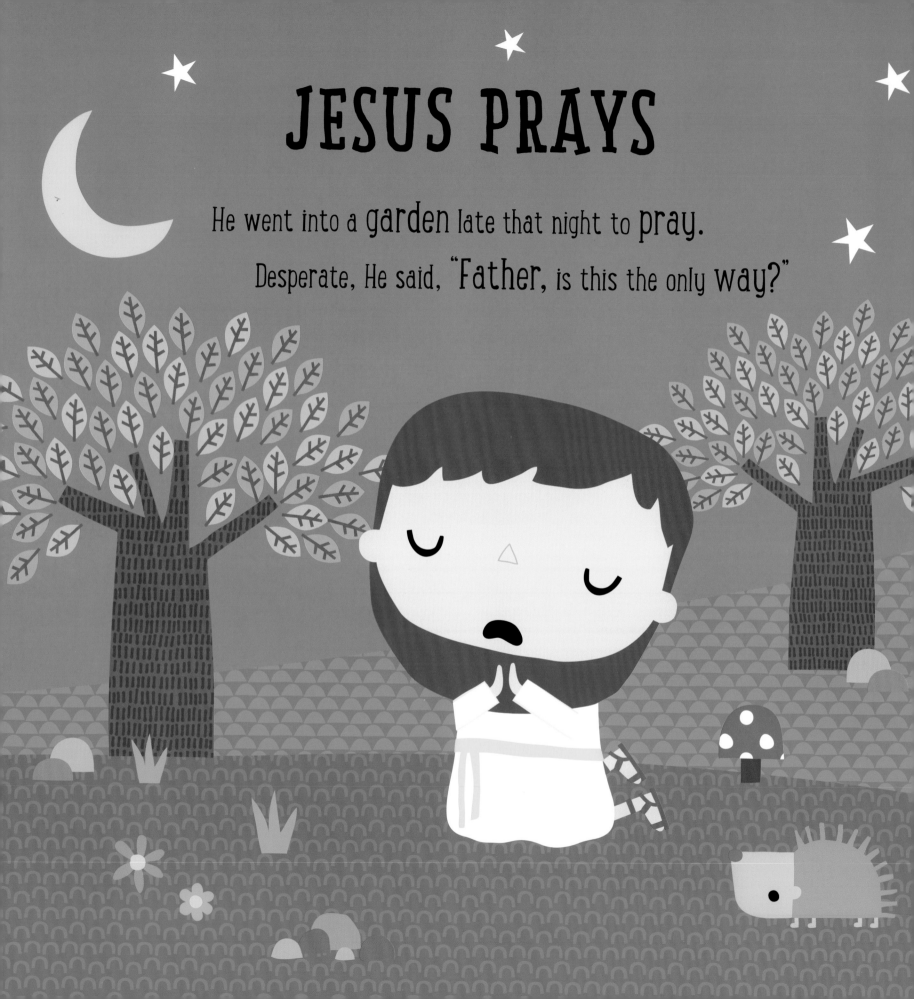

JESUS IS ARRESTED

The men who hated Jesus found Him **praying** there.

They took Him to be **judged** even though it was not **fair**.

JESUS IS QUESTIONED

They asked Jesus **questions** for a very long time
but could not find Him **guilty** of a **single** crime.
When the ruler called **Pilate** wished to set Jesus **free**,
many in the crowd **shouted**, "Hang Him on a tree!"

THE CRUCIFIXION

Jesus was **not** guilty, but He was put on a **cross**.

Just as God had **told** Him: His life must be **lost**.

JESUS IS BURIED

Suddenly the sky went **dark** and everyone was **scared**.

Six hours later, Jesus **died**, and all His friends despaired.

Some men took His **body** and put it in a cave.

They rolled a stone across to make a sealed **grave**.

JESUS IS ALIVE!

On the **third** day, to their **surprise**,

the stone had rolled away, and Jesus was **alive!**

HOPE FOR US ALL

And all this was God's plan: that Jesus had to die

to pay the price for sin, for all our wrongs and lies.

And so, because of Jesus, when our lives are through,

we can live in heaven if we trust and love Him too.